WHY DO PEOPLE HAVE
CHINS?

AND OTHER CURIOUS HUMAN ADAPTATIONS

BY PATRICIA FLETCHER

Gareth Stevens
PUBLISHING

Please visit our website, www.garethstevens.com. For a free color catalog of all our high-quality books, call toll free 1-800-542-2595 or fax 1-877-542-2596.

Cataloging-in-Publication Data

Names: Fletcher, Patricia.
Title: Why do people have chins? And other curious human adaptations / Patricia Fletcher.
Description: New York : Gareth Stevens Publishing, 2018. | Series: Odd adaptations | Includes index.
Identifiers: ISBN 9781538203972 (pbk.) | ISBN 9781538203996 (library bound) | ISBN 9781538203989 (6 pack)
Subjects: LCSH: Human body–Juvenile literature. | Human biology–Juvenile literature. | Adaptation (Biology)–Juvenile literature.
Classification: LCC QP37.F54 2018 | DDC 612–dc23

First Edition

Published in 2018 by
Gareth Stevens Publishing
111 East 14th Street, Suite 349
New York, NY 10003

Copyright © 2018 Gareth Stevens Publishing

Designer: Sarah Liddell
Editor: Kristen Nelson

Photo credits: Cover, p. 1 Jo millington/Shutterstock.com; background used throughout Captblack76/Shutterstock.com; p. 4 Samuel Borges Photography/Shutterstock.com; p. 5 Rawpixel.com/Shutterstock.com; p. 6 TOM MCHUGH/ Getty Images; p. 7 (left) ESB Professional/Shutterstock.com; p. 7 (right) Wally Stemberger/Shutterstock.com; p. 9 Monkey Business Images/Shutterstock.com; p. 10 E R DEGGINGER/Getty Images; p. 11 CLIPAREA/ Shutterstock.com; p. 12 (both) Dorling Kindersley/Getty Images; p. 13 Radu Bercan/Shutterstock.com; p. 14 Nicholas Veasey/Getty Images; p. 15 Albina Glisic/Shutterstock.com; p. 16 Laurent Renault/Shutterstock.com; p. 17 Suttha Burawonk/Shutterstock.com; p. 18 aslysun/Shutterstock.com; p. 19 (thoughtful) Asier Romero/Shutterstock.com; p. 19 (surprised) Syda Productions/Shutterstock.com; p. 19 (mad) FabrikaSimf/Shutterstock.com; p. 19 (scared) pathdoc/Shutterstock.com; p. 20 Roger Jegg - Fotodesign-Jegg.de/Shutterstock.com; p. 21 KBF Media/ Shutterstock.com; p. 22 aaabbbccc/Shutterstock.com; p. 23 Mandavi/Wikimedia Commons; p. 24 kenary820/ Shutterstock.com; p. 25 Have a nice day Photo/Shutterstock.com; p. 29 (top left) PHAS/Contributor/Universal Images Group/Getty Images; p. 29 (top right) SHEILA TERRY/SCIENCE PHOTO LIBRARY/Getty Images; p. 29 (bottom) Universal History Archive/Contributor/Universal Images Group/Getty Images.

CONTENTS

Words in the glossary appear in **bold** type the first time they are used in the text.

CHIN UP!

What sets humans apart from other animals? **ONE WEIRD FEATURE IS THAT HUMANS HAVE AN ODD BUMP OF BONE ON THEIR LOWER JAW—A CHIN!** No other animals on Earth have it! Even odder, no one is totally sure why we have it. Popular **theories** that it's an adaptation that helps us chew or speak were proven wrong.

One theory that seems likely to some scientists is that humans used to have very large, strong jaws for chewing. As our jaws got smaller over time, the bone we call a chin may have become easier to see.

ADAPTATION EXPLANATION

Adaptations are changes in animals' bodies or behaviors in order to better survive in their **environment**. When an environment faces change, such as getting colder, animals that are better at dealing with that change survive more often than others. **OVER MANY GENERATIONS, THE TRAITS, OR FEATURES, THAT HELPED SURVIVAL ARE PASSED DOWN, CREATING A LASTING CHANGE IN THE POPULATION—AN ADAPTATION!**

THE HUMAN CHIN IS
ONE OF MANY WEIRD BODY
ADAPTATIONS THAT SCIENTISTS
AREN'T QUITE SURE WHY
WE **DEVELOPED!**

5

ALWAYS EVOLVING

The process of animals—including people—changing over time is called evolution. **ADAPTATION IS A KEY PART OF EVOLUTION!**

Early members of our species of human, *Homo sapiens*, lived in Africa. Their bodies were adapted to live in that climate. Then, about 100,000 years ago, *Homo sapiens* began to spread out. Over thousands of years, they began to live in many different climates and conditions all over the world. **THE NEW ENVIRONMENTS DROVE LOTS OF ADAPTATIONS, INCLUDING CHANGES IN SKIN COLOR, BODY SHAPE, AND EVEN NOSE SHAPE!** As these adaptations were passed down from parents to children, *Homo sapiens'* DNA changed. It continues to change today!

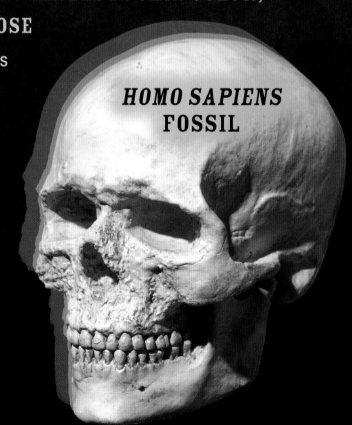

HOMO SAPIENS FOSSIL

MUCH OF WHAT WE KNOW ABOUT ADAPTATIONS IN *HOMO SAPIENS* HAS BEEN LEARNED FROM FOSSILS, SUCH AS THIS SKULL, WHICH MIGHT BE AS MUCH AS ABOUT 40,000 YEARS OLD.

LET'S BE NOSE-Y!

In hot, wet climates, peoples' noses have evolved to be wider and flatter. This allows air that's breathed in to be moist and to keep that moisture in the body when the air is breathed out. In cold, dry places, small, long, and narrow noses make the air breathed in warmer and wetter!

KEEPING WARM, KEEPING COOL

Typical human bodies share the same features: two arms and two legs; a **torso**; and a head with two eyes, a nose, and two ears. But have you ever thought about how different people can look? **SOME BODY DIFFERENCES CAN BE LINKED TO ADAPTATIONS FOR EXTREME TEMPERATURES!**

Short, rounder bodies are well adapted to live in the cold. Other cold adaptations include flat faces, short arms and legs, and often more body fat. These adaptations help people lose less heat. Areas where the weather is hot and wet favor people who are tall and thin. They're better able to let out the heat!

HERE COMES THE SUN

SKIN COLOR IS AN ADAPTATION TO CLIMATE, TOO! In hot regions, darker skin developed as protection against the sun's harmful rays. In cold regions that may have periods with little or no sun, people developed lighter skin to allow the sun's rays to enter their skin and help their body make vitamin D.

MANY PHYSICAL ADAPTATIONS, SUCH AS BODY SHAPE, LIKELY DEVELOPED AS A RESULT OF THE CLIMATE IN WHICH A GROUP OF PEOPLE LIVED.

THE SHRINKING BRAIN

Do you think humans today are smarter than our **ancestors**? Scientists can't measure ancient humans' intelligence, but they can measure their skull size to find out how big their brains were. **THAT'S LED TO A SURPRISING CONCLUSION—HUMANS TODAY HAVE THE SMALLEST BRAINS OF ANY OF OUR SPECIES IN THE LAST 100,000 YEARS!**

For a long time, the human brain was getting bigger. Why it started to shrink is still unknown. Some scientists think though the brain is smaller, it's more **efficient**. Others think the smaller brain is because our bodies have also gotten smaller over time.

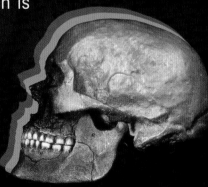

CRO-MAGNON SKULL FOSSIL

TENNIS, ANYONE?

Anthropologists study fossils and other early human remains to learn how brain size has changed over time. The Cro-Magnons—*Homo sapiens* who lived about 30,000 to 20,000 years ago—had the biggest brain among our ancestors. **TODAY, THE HUMAN BRAIN IS *SMALLER* THAN THE CRO-MAGNON BRAIN BY ABOUT AS MUCH AS A TENNIS BALL!**

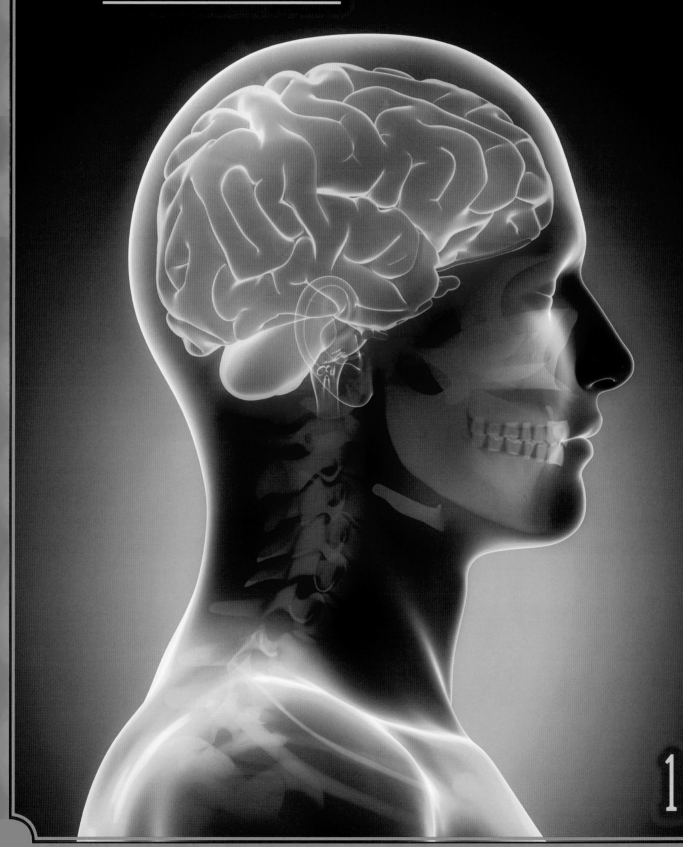

DON'T WORRY—A
SMALLER BRAIN DOESN'T
NECESSARILY MEAN HUMANS
ARE GETTING DUMBER!

11

SINK YOUR TEETH IN

AS OUR BODIES HAVE GOTTEN SMALLER, OUR MOUTHS MAY HAVE GOTTEN TOO SMALL! Many people don't have room in their mouth for the third set of **molars** often called wisdom teeth. That's another result of our jaw adapting and becoming considerably smaller than our ancestors' jaw. Human teeth have gotten much smaller over the last 2 million years or so, too. What caused these adaptations?

It's likely human jaws and teeth evolved to be smaller than our ancestors' because humans began to use tools and cook their food! The powerful jaws and large teeth were no longer needed.

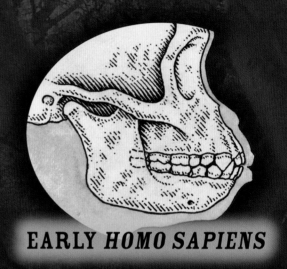

EARLY *HOMO SAPIENS*

MODERN HUMAN

THESE ILLUSTRATIONS SHOW THE ADAPTATIONS OF JAWS AND TEETH OF *HOMO SAPIENS* OVER THOUSANDS OF YEARS!

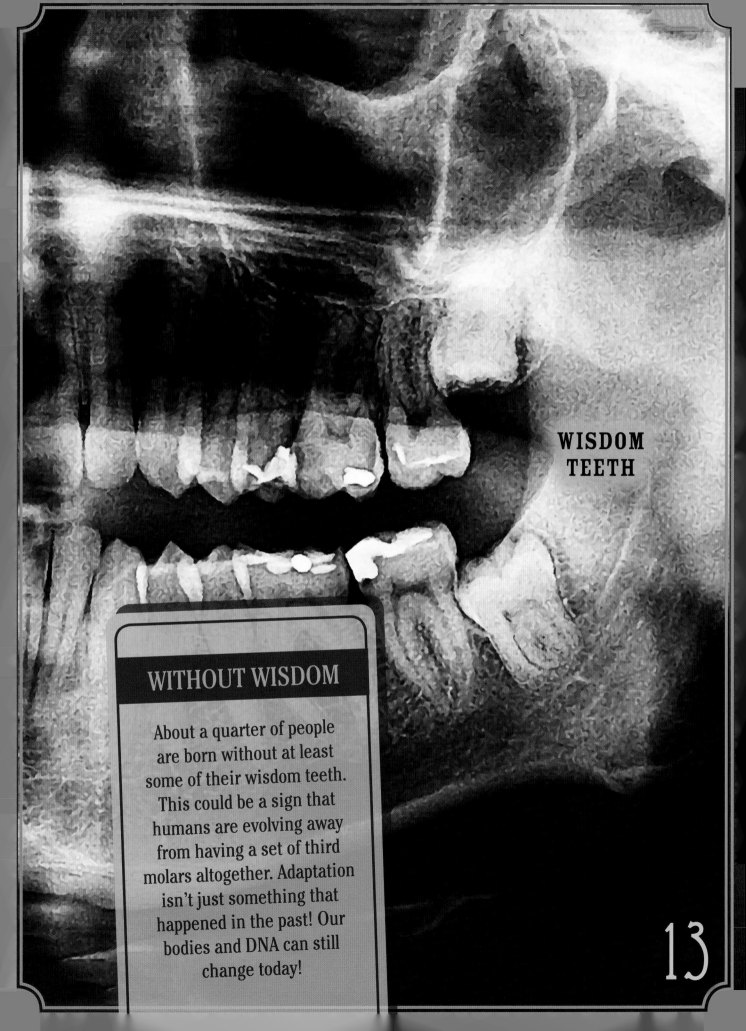

WISDOM TEETH

WITHOUT WISDOM

About a quarter of people are born without at least some of their wisdom teeth. This could be a sign that humans are evolving away from having a set of third molars altogether. Adaptation isn't just something that happened in the past! Our bodies and DNA can still change today!

13

MADE FOR WALKING?

To us, walking on two legs is normal. But when thinking about the whole animal kingdom, walking on two legs is a pretty odd adaptation. Walking on two legs is called bipedalism (by-PEH-duhl-ih-zuhm). **BEFORE ABOUT 4 MILLION YEARS AGO, HUMAN ANCESTORS MOVED USING THEIR FEET AND THEIR HANDS!**

Anthropologists have many theories about why humans became bipedal. Our ancestors may have moved onto grasslands from forests and needed to be able to see long distances better. Walking on two legs also takes a lot less energy and frees up hands and arms to carry things and use tools.

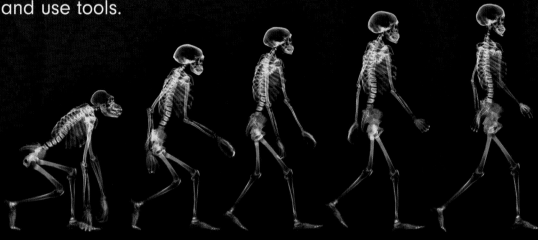

THESE SKELETONS SHOW THE EVOLUTION OF OUR HUMAN ANCESTORS FROM WALKING ON ALL FOURS TO BIPEDALISM. IF YOU LOOK CLOSELY, YOU CAN SEE THE LENGTH AND SHAPE OF THE ARMS CHANGED, TOO! SOMETIMES, ADAPTATIONS CAUSE OTHER ADAPTATIONS!

INCOMPLETE ADAPTATION

What's even stranger is that even though humans have been bipedal for millions of years, our bodies haven't fully adapted! Our backs and knees, which are commonly injured areas in humans, still aren't formed the best they can be to carry a person's upper body weight. Evolution sure moves slowly!

15

YOU WOULD STILL BE ABLE TO WALK WITHOUT YOUR PINKY TOE! In fact, some people barely have pinky toes already. It's one feature of the human body that's being lost as we adapt to our present conditions.

Human ancestors used their feet to climb trees and grab. Today, we don't need our toes for that! What we do need are our metatarsals, or the bones that connect our toes to our ankle. Human feet have five metatarsals in all. The most important parts of our feet for balance are the fifth metatarsal, the first metatarsal (for the big toe), and our heel.

MONKEY FEET

Human ancestors are related to ancestors of apes and monkeys, which are all in an animal group called primates. Yet our feet look nothing like theirs! Over time, the human foot adapted to walking and balancing, while primates' feet are still used to climb and grab tree branches. **THE HUMAN FOOTPRINT IS UNIQUE TO OUR SPECIES!**

TOES

METATARSALS

HEEL

WOULD YOUR FEET
LOOK WEIRD WITHOUT
THE PINKY TOES?

17

BROW ARE YOU?

The color of your hair and how much you have are written in your DNA! Some people have a lot of body hair—but no one today has as much body hair as our distant ancestors! Over time, we've adapted to having most of our hair on top of our head. It protects us from the sun and keeps us warm!

OTHER HAIR ON OUR BODY HAS A PURPOSE, TOO—EVEN EYEBROWS! Eyebrows keep sweat and water out of our eyes. Eyebrows are also one of the main ways other people know how we feel.

DON'T BLINK!

For a long time, scientists didn't know why humans evolved to have eyelashes. In 2015, a study seemed to say that eyelashes change the airflow near the human eye. That means eyelashes keep dust and harmful matter out of the eye while keeping the eye moist!

YOUR EYEBROWS CAN TALK!

THOUGHTFUL

SURPRISED

MAD

SCARED

THESE PHOTOS SHOW HOW EYEBROWS
HELP SHOW OTHERS WHAT YOU'RE
FEELING, EVEN IF YOU AREN'T TALKING!

19

When you're nervous, you might feel your face and neck get hot. **BLUSHING, OR YOUR FACE TURNING RED, IS A STRANGE ADAPTATION UNIQUE TO HUMANS!**

Blushing might seem upsetting when it happens. But it's a way for you to show people angry with you that you feel bad without saying anything. Scientists have found that people are more **sympathetic** to a person who blushes in response to something than to someone who stays cool under the pressure. Blushing is an involuntary response, which means you didn't choose to do it. That means there's no doubt you're being totally honest!

Blushing may have evolved because groups of people follow social cues. A person blushing shows they know deep inside they've done something outside their social code. This makes sense, since children seem to start blushing around the time they become aware of the people around them.

BLUSHING IS CAUSED BY THE BODY RELEASING THE **HORMONE** ADRENALINE. THE ADRENALINE CAUSES MORE BLOOD TO FLOW TO YOUR FACE, MAKING IT APPEAR RED.

21

AT ALTITUDE

Denver, Colorado, is called the Mile High City because it's about 1 mile (1.6 km) above sea level. If you visit there, you might get winded more easily because there's less oxygen the higher you are above sea level and humans can't breathe as well.

The people living atop the Tibetan Plateau of Asia have adapted to life more than 14,000 feet (4,267 m) above sea level in a pretty cool way. **THEY'RE ABLE TO BETTER USE A GAS CALLED NITRIC OXIDE, WHICH WIDENS THEIR BLOOD VESSELS TO ALLOW FOR BETTER BLOOD FLOW.** They also take more breaths per minute than people living at sea level.

BODY CHANGES THAT ALLOW TIBETANS TO LIVE SO HIGH ABOVE SEA LEVEL ARE ODD, BUT NECESSARY, ADAPTATIONS.

TIBETAN PLATEAU

ANDES ADAPTATION

Those living high on the Andean plateau in South America have adapted to life above 12,000 feet (3,658 m), too. **THE ANDEANS' RED BLOOD CELLS HAVE ADAPTED TO CARRY MORE OXYGEN IN THEIR BLOOD THAN ANYONE LIVING AT SEA LEVEL!** This means they're more efficient breathers than most people!

ANDEAN PLATEAU

HANDY NAILS

Fingernails help us when we itch...but what else are they good for? **FINGERNAILS MAY HAVE REPLACED CLAWS IN OUR PRIMATE ANCESTORS MILLIONS OF YEARS AGO!** Today, having fingernails instead of claws is one major difference between primates, such as humans, and other mammals.

FINGERNAILS MAY BE A SIDE EFFECT OF ANOTHER ADAPTATION. More than 2 million years ago, primates started to develop wider fingertips. Fingernails may have been part of this change and may help protect important finger bones. This adaptation might have helped primates move better in treetops as well.

UNHEALTHY NAIL

NAILS AND HEALTH

Today, fingernails have proved to be an important adaptation that can show a person's health. Someone who doesn't have a balanced, healthy diet can have discolored nails or nails that break very easily. Your nails can show signs of certain illnesses, too. One sign of heart problems is nails that are pale or bluish.

FINGERNAILS ALSO HELP US GRAB BETTER AND USE TOOLS, SO THAT'S ANOTHER POSSIBLE REASON THIS ADAPTATION HAS STAYED WITH US!

25

One of humanity's oddest adaptations is something we do every day: talking! No other species in the animal kingdom communicates the way we do.

It gets even stranger. **SCIENTISTS AREN'T SURE WHEN PEOPLE STARTED TALKING TO ONE ANOTHER.** A recent study concluded it may have been about 1.75 million years ago, but other scientists believe it was at least 2 million years ago. Still more think speech is a recent adaptation that happened 50,000 years ago!

It's hard to date when humans started speaking because the body parts used for speech, such as the tongue and voice box, don't fossilize.

NO NEED TO ADAPT

Many adaptations are biological, meaning they're changes having to do with the body. **SOMETIMES, HUMAN INVENTIONS HAVE ALLOWED US TO SURVIVE WITHOUT NEEDING TO BIOLOGICALLY ADAPT!** For example, while in the past people with more fat would naturally survive better in cold climates, today, someone tall and thin could simply wear a warmer coat!

TIMELINE OF TALK

BIRTH-3 MONTHS
BABIES CRY TO COMMUNICATE WHEN THEY'RE HUNGRY OR TIRED OR TO SHOW OTHER NEEDS. THEY START TO RECOGNIZE VOICES AND CALM DOWN WHEN SOMEONE THEY KNOW SPEAKS TO THEM.

4-6 MONTHS
BABIES CAN MAKE SOME SOUNDS, INCLUDING THOSE THAT START WITH P, B, AND M, AND MAY BABBLE WHEN FEELING UNHAPPY OR EXCITED.

7 MONTHS-1 YEAR
BABIES START TO UNDERSTAND COMMON, FAMILIAR WORDS. THEY COPY SOUNDS OF SPEECH AND MAY SPEAK ONE OR TWO WORDS BY THE TIME THEY ARE 1.

1 YEAR-2 YEARS
BABIES LEARN NEW WORDS OFTEN AND START TO PUT THEM TOGETHER INTO PHRASES AND SHORT QUESTIONS.

2-3 YEARS
CHILDREN CAN SPEAK IN TWO- AND THREE-WORD PHRASES AND CAN BE UNDERSTOOD BY THEIR FAMILY.

3-4 YEARS
CHILDREN CAN USE SENTENCES OF FOUR OR MORE WORDS TO TALK ABOUT THEIR DAY AND ANSWER SIMPLE QUESTIONS.

DO YOU REMEMBER YOUR FIRST WORDS? YOU PROBABLY WERE TOO YOUNG! THIS TIMELINE SHOWS ABOUT WHEN THE AVERAGE CHILD BEGINS TO DEVELOP LANGUAGE.

4-5 YEARS
CHILDREN CAN UNDERSTAND MOST OF WHAT IS SPOKEN TO THEM AS WELL AS TELL THEIR OWN STORIES TO OTHERS.

SHORT-TERM ADAPTATION

In order for something to be called an evolutionary adaptation, it has to be something that can be passed down from parents to children. These changes are commonly long lasting and take a long time to spread across a population.

HUMANS ADAPT TO THEIR SURROUNDINGS IN OTHER, SHORT-TERM WAYS, TOO. THESE ADJUSTMENTS TO NEW CONDITIONS ARE OFTEN REVERSIBLE. Being able to easily adapt to new surroundings is an adaptation, too! And those who easily adapt are more likely to survive long enough to pass on their genes. That means they're more likely to help shape future human adaptations!

ON THE CELLULAR LEVEL

Certain kinds of doctors that spend a lot of time around X-rays appear to be adapting to deal with the extra radiation. In a small study, their blood had high levels of matter caused by radiation that could be harmful. They also had high levels of the body's cell protectors, antioxidants. Could this be an adaptation in the making?

TOOL FROM
AROUND 6000 BC

TOOLS FROM
2000-1700 BC

ARTIFACTS ARE THE OBJECTS
USED BY PEOPLE IN THE
PAST. THEY CAN TELL US A LOT
ABOUT WHAT LIFE WAS LIKE
DURING A CERTAIN TIME,
AS WELL AS SHOW US HOW
HUMANS EVOLVED!

HAMMERS FROM
ANCIENT ROME

29

GLOSSARY

ancestor: an animal that lived before others in its family tree

anthropologist: someone who studies humans and their societies

develop: to grow and change

efficient: having to do with the most effective or purposeful way of doing something

environment: the conditions that surround a living thing and affect the way it lives

extreme: very great

hormone: a chemical made in the body that tells another part of the body what to do

molar: a broad, flat tooth made for grinding food

radiation: waves of energy

reversible: able to be reversed, or turned back to an earlier state

sympathetic: having feelings of kind acceptance

theory: an explanation based on facts that is generally accepted by scientists

torso: the trunk of the body

unique: one of a kind

FOR MORE INFORMATION

BOOKS

Heos, Bridget. *Shell, Beak, Tusk: Shared Traits and the Wonders of Adaptation*. Boston, MA: Houghton Mifflin Harcourt, 2017.

National Geographic. *Weird but True Human Body*. Washington, DC: National Geographic, 2017.

WEBSITES

Animal Adaptations
ecokids.ca/swf-files/gamesPage/adaptations.swf
Play a game to test your knowledge of animal adaptations!

Animal Adaptations for Kids
easyscienceforkids.com/animal-adaptations-for-kids-video-for-kids/
Watch a video about adaptations here to learn more!

Human Body
easyscienceforkids.com/human-body/
Find out even more about how the human body works on this website.

Publisher's note to educators and parents: Our editors have carefully reviewed these websites to ensure that they are suitable for students. Many websites change frequently, however, and we cannot guarantee that a site's future contents will continue to meet our high standards of quality and educational value. Be advised that students should be closely supervised whenever they access the Internet.

31

INDEX